Christian Church

For Jennifer, Caroline, David, and Joshua

For a free color catalog describing Gareth Stevens' list of high-quality books and multimedia programs, call 1-800-542-2595 (USA) or 1-800-461-9120 (Canada). Gareth Stevens Publishing's Fax: (414) 225-0377.

Library of Congress Cataloging-in-Publication Data available upon request from publisher.
Fax: (414) 225-0377 for the attention of the Publishing Records Department.

ISBN 0-8368-2606-X

This North American edition first published in 2000 by
Gareth Stevens Publishing
1555 North RiverCenter Drive, Suite 201
Milwaukee, WI 53212 USA

Original edition © 1998 by Franklin Watts.
First published in 1998 by Franklin Watts,
96 Leonard Street, London EC2A 4RH, England.
This U. S. edition © 2000 by Gareth Stevens, Inc.
Additional end matter © 2000 by Gareth Stevens, Inc.

Editor: Samantha Armstrong
Series Designer: Kirstie Billingham
Illustrator: Gemini Patel
Religious Education Consultant: Margaret Barratt, M.A., Religious Education Lecturer
Christianity Consultant: Alison Seaman, Deputy Director, National Society Religious Education Centre
Reading Consultant: Prue Goodwin, Reading and Language Information Centre, Reading

Gareth Stevens Series Editor: Dorothy L. Gibbs

Photographic acknowledgements:
Cover: Steve Shott Photography; Sonia Halliday and Laura Lushington.
Inside: p. 6 Nicholas Kane/Arcaid; p. 9 (left) Angela Wood; p. 9 (right) Carlos Reyes-Manzo, Andes Press Agency; p. 10 Mohamad Ansar, Impact; p. 14 Mohamad Ansar, Impact; p. 15 Sonia Halliday and Laura Lushington; p. 16 H. Rogers, Trip Photographic Library; p. 17 The Methodist Church, Camberwell; p. 18 Carlos Reyes-Manzo, Andes Press Agency; p. 26 John Fryer, Circa Photo Library; p. 27 (left) Mark Cator, Impact. All other photographs by Steve Shott Photography.

With thanks to the Russian Patriarchal Cathedral of the Dormiton and All Saints, The Church of Our Lady, Camberwell Methodist Church, and St. Edwards RC Primary School.

Printed in the United States of America

1 2 3 4 5 6 7 8 9 04 03 02 01 00

Christian
Church

Angela Wood

Gareth Stevens Publishing
MILWAUKEE

The cross is a symbol used to represent the Christian faith.

Contents

Words that appear in the glossary are printed in **boldface**
type the first time they occur in the text.

Churches around the World

A **church** is a place where Christians meet to **worship God**. There are many different kinds of Christian worship, and there are churches all around the world.

This modern church ▶ is in England.

Christian Beliefs

Christians believe in one God who created the world. God loved people so much that he sent his son, Jesus, to live among them.

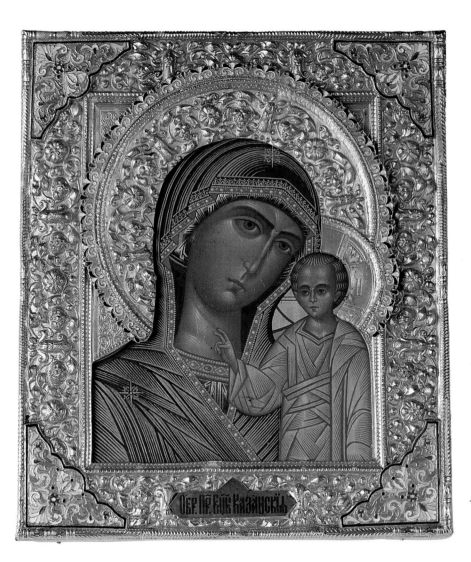

◀ This is Jesus with his mother, Mary.

7

Jesus

Jesus lived on Earth and helped people understand about God. He taught them how to live together in a loving way. Because many people did not understand who Jesus was or the things he did, he was killed on a **cross**. Some churches have a statue of Jesus on the cross. It is called a **crucifix**.

When Christians see a ▶ crucifix, they remember that Jesus loved them enough to die for them.

Many churches have a plain cross, instead of a crucifix. Christians believe that, three days after he was buried, Jesus was alive again and with his followers. The plain cross reminds Christians that Jesus did not die forever and that he will always be with them.

Churches often have ▶ candles in them. They help Christians remember that Jesus was like a light to guide them.

9

Inside a Church

A church can be plain inside, or it can have many religious pictures and objects. A **priest**, minister, or preacher usually leads the worship **service** from the front of the church.

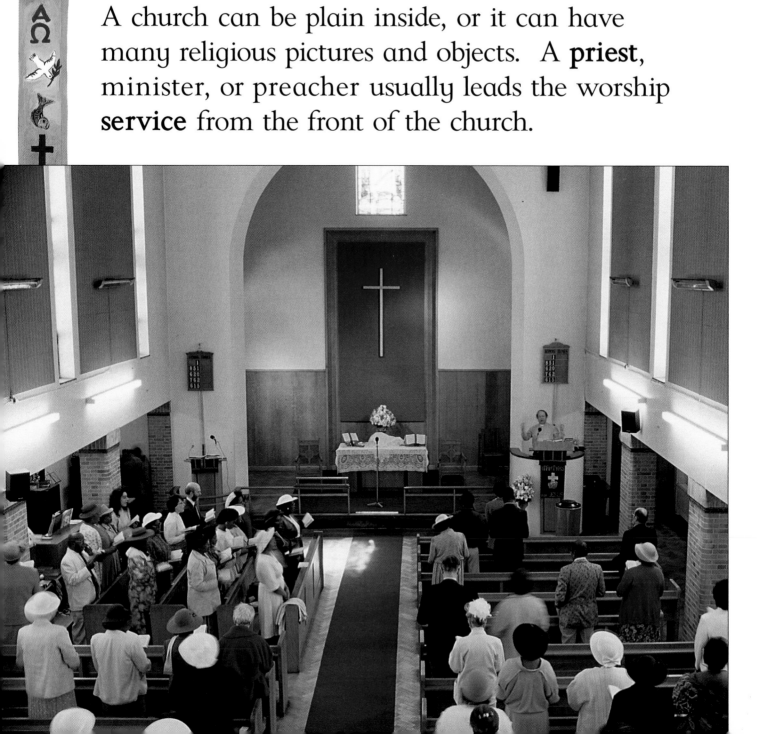

The Altar

Most churches have an **altar** or a communion table at the front or in a place where everyone can see it. The altar is like the table at which Jesus had the last meal with his followers. At this meal, called the Last Supper, Jesus told his followers he would always be with them.

◀ There is often a cross or a candle on the altar or communion table.

THE LORD OF ALL GOOD LIFE

The Bible

The **Bible** is the most important Christian book. It tells how God guided people before Jesus was born. It also describes Jesus, his teachings, and the beginning of the church. There almost always are Bibles in a church, and many Christians have their own Bibles.

◀ This Orthodox minister, or deacon, is reading the Bible to the **congregation**.

The Bible is often ▶ read from a stand called a lectern. This priest is kissing the Bible to show his love and **respect** for God's words.

The Sermon

During a service, the preacher usually explains what the Bible means to Christians today. This talk is called a sermon.

The sermon helps ▶ Christians think about what they believe.

Windows

Some churches have beautiful windows with pictures made of stained glass. The pictures often tell stories from the Bible or show **saints**. Saints are people who led good and **holy** lives and did special things out of love for Jesus.

This stained-glass ▶ window shows Jesus with Saint John the Baptist.

Being Part of the Church

People usually start life as a Christian by being **baptized**, which means they are **blessed** with holy water. At a church, the holy water is often kept in a **font**.

This woman is in a Catholic church. ▶
She is going to bless herself with holy water from the small font on the wall.

◀ Christians can be baptized either as babies or when they are grown up. This baby is being baptized at a special baptismal font.

Christians feel that God is always with them. They call this feeling the Holy Spirit. The Holy Spirit shows people how to love and help others. In most churches, the Holy Spirit is shown as a dove or a flame.

One way Christians help others is by ▶ giving money to those in need. The money is often collected in church.

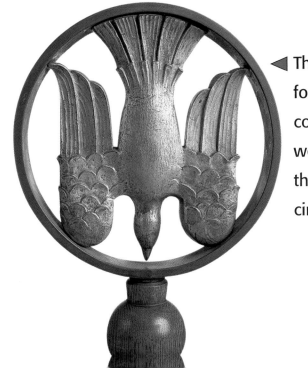

◀ This symbol stands for the Holy Spirit coming into the world. The dove is the Holy Spirit. The circle is the world.

17

 # A Church Service

The special day for most Christians is Sunday. Many churches have services on Sunday. At a service, Christians come together to share their love for God. In some churches, there are lots of people at the service, and music plays an important part. In others, the service is very quiet and still.

These children are sitting together in church as they pray to God.

As part of a service, people say **prayers**. Prayers are one way Christians speak to and hear God. Often, someone reads from the Bible at a service, and everyone joins in the singing of **hymns** that praise God. In some churches, a **choir** leads the singing.

Holy Communion

During a service, some churches have **Holy Communion** to remember Jesus' Last Supper with his followers. The minister or priest blesses pieces of bread and some wine or grape juice for people to eat and drink.

When people eat and drink the bread and wine,
they think about how much Jesus loves them.

Mass

In some churches, such as Roman Catholic churches, the service is called a **mass**. Holy Communion is given at the mass. The priest uses a special kind of bread shaped like a wafer. Each wafer is called a **host**.

Children often ▶ help the priest at the altar during a mass.

◀ Hosts are kept behind the altar in a place called the tabernacle.

Praying Alone

Sometimes Christians pray quietly to God on their own. Praying alone gives them a chance to think about what God means to them.

This man is praying in front ▶
of a religious picture called
an **icon**. He is making the
sign of the cross on his body.

◀ This woman is lighting
a candle and saying a
prayer while she kneels
in front of a statue of Jesus.

25

Children in a Church

In most churches, children can take part in many different activities. For example, they can go to classes, where they hear stories from the Bible and learn about being Christians.

◀ These children are making models as part of learning about a story from the Bible.

◀ Children can belong
to the church choir.

Children often read ▶
from the Bible during
a church service.

Glossary

altar: a large table in a church on which a worship service is celebrated.

baptized: became a member of the Christian church by being blessed with holy water.

Bible: the special and most important book for Christians.

blessed: made holy; given or shown God's love and care in a special way.

choir: a group of singers in a church or at a religious service.

church: the place where Christians meet to worship God.

congregation: the people who belong to a church or are together in a church for a service.

cross: a symbol of the Christian church because Jesus died on one.

crucifix: a cross that has the image of Jesus on it to remind Christians of his love for them.

font: a bowl that holds holy water for a baptism or blessings.

God: Creator of the universe and the highest, most powerful being, known by Christians as the Father, the Son, and the Holy Spirit.

holy: especially close to God; blessed by God.

Holy Communion: the offering of bread and wine during a Christian worship service.

host: a small, thin, flat, round piece of a special kind of bread.

hymns: songs sung to praise God.

icon: a religious picture or image.

mass: a worship service for Catholics and some other Christians.

prayers: the words people say or think when they speak to God.

priest: (*also*, minister or preacher) a person who leads a Christian worship service.

respect: to treat with honor and thoughtful consideration.

saints: people who have shown a special love for God by living good and holy lives.

service: a meeting of Christians in church to worship God.

worship: to show love and respect with prayer, usually as part of a religious service.

More Books to Read

Being a Christian: A Study Book for Children. David Walters (Good News Fellowship Ministries)

A Child's First Catholic Dictionary. Thomas Mustachio (Ave Maria Press)

An Easter Celebration. Pamela Kennedy (Ideals)

I Am Protestant and *I Am Roman Catholic. Religions of the World* (series). Philemon D. Sevastiades (Rosen/ Powerkids Press)

I Want to Know about the Church. I Want to Know (series). Rick Osborne (Zondervan Publishing House)

Lives and Legends of the Saints: With Paintings from the Great Art Museums of the World. Carole Armstrong (Simon and Schuster)

My Big Family at Church. Growing in Faith (series). Helen Rayburn Caswell (Abingdon Press)

A Peek into My Church. Wendy Goody (Whippersnapper Books)

Pioneer Church. Carolyn Otto (Henry Holt and Company)

The Sacraments. Inos Biffi (William B. Eerdmans Publishing)

Videos

The Beginner's Bible.
Jesus and His Miracles.
(Sony Wonder)

Greatest Adventure Stories
from the Bible (series).
(Turner Home Video)

The Mass for Children.
(Oblate Media and
Communication)

The Story Keepers (series).
(Oblate Media and
Communication)

Web Sites

Bible Stories for Kids.
www.misslink.org/
children/bibstory.html

Children's Bible Hour: How
to Become a Child of God
www.gospelcom.net/
cbh/child.shtml

Church Kids!
www.virtualchurch.org/
kids.htm

Kids' Quest
www.ChristianAnswers.
net/kids/home.html

To find additional web sites, use a reliable search engine with
one or more of the following keywords: *baptism, Bible,*
Christian, Christianity, church, communion, God, Holy Spirit,
Jesus, prayer, and *saints.*

Index